MW01504805

THE SUN & THE MOON.

THE SUN & THE MOON.

KRISTINA MARIE DARLING

BLAZEVOX[BOOKS]
Buffalo, New York

THE SUN & THE MOON
by Kristina Marie Darling

Copyright © 2014

Published by BlazeVOX [books]

All rights reserved. No part of this book may be reproduced without
the publisher's written permission, except for brief quotations in reviews.

Printed in the United States of America

Interior design and typesetting by Geoffrey Gatza
Cover Art by

First Edition
ISBN: 978-1-60964-191-7
Library of Congress Control Number: 2014949805

BlazeVOX [books]
131 Euclid Ave
Kenmore, NY 14217

Editor@blazevox.org

publisher of weird little books

BlazeVOX [books]

blazevox.org

21 20 19 18 17 16 15 14 13 12 01 02 03 04 05 06 07 08 09 10

BlazeVOX

ACKNOWLEDGEMENTS.

Thank you to the Ragdale Foundation for their generous support during the time this book was written. The author would also like to thank her family for their ongoing support of her writing.

CONTENTS.

THE SUN & THE MOON.

(I)

You began as a small mark on the horizon. Then night &
its endless train of ghosts. You led them in, one after the
other. They took off their shoes, hung their coats &
started looking through the drawers. By then I could
hardly speak. I realized the lock on the door must not be
working. The floor was covered in ash. There was
nothing I could do, so I kept trying to tell you goodnight.
You just stood there, your hands in your pockets, that
small army behind you. That was when they started
polishing the knives.

(II)

At first, you told me the knives weren't what they seemed. Pearl-handled, wrapped in blue paper & engraved with our initials, you had presented them as a gift. But sometimes things go wrong at parties. Before we know it, the ghosts are fighting over the gift wrap, tearing ribbons from each of the boxes. I beg them not to, but there's nothing that can be done. Everyone starts throwing their drinks on the fire. Soon the house is burning all around us. You turn to me & say it looks a little more like daylight.

(III)

Even when I said the fires were too much, I loved the way the flames lit your face from the ashes below. Ablaze & shimmering, you'd watch as the party grew smaller & the room brighter. One by one the ghosts left for the ocean, dragging those cold dark stars behind them. The house was nearly empty. When you closed the door for the last time, I could only stare. The tablecloth was burning & still you just sat there, stoking that enormous fire. That's when I turn to you & ask if daylight always looks this way.

(IV)

The next morning, those remnants of the party were everywhere: torn curtains, a broken window, my violet nightdress hanging from the chandelier. Still you slept & slept, your eyes like cold stars in a locked box. Now light pours in through every window & I realize that you aren't going to wake up anytime soon. It's the strangest things that keep me from leaving. I begin circling around you, waving my arms, shouting your name as though it had been a secret. Somehow you keep dreaming, heaving that frozen sky behind you.

(V)

Some days I wonder what you're doing with the ghosts. They come & go as they please, fumbling with our gate in the middle of the night. Eventually I asked where you found them, but you insisted they found us. Yes, they followed you to the door, unfurled my silver hairpin & picked the lock. You said you'd already warned them, shaking that empty wine bottle in the air. But at the same time, I was sure you remembered them from before. I realized how little I knew about our house & those elaborate silver traps you kept beside the gate.

(VI)

A few days later, the ghosts were back. I saw them opening windows, waiting at the kitchen table, gazing into the little mirror above my armoire. By then I could barely speak. The floor was covered in soot. You begin carrying them out, one by one, closing the door behind you. But I remembered the night we last saw them, trembling in the cellar, that cold light gathering all around us. So I nod my head & tell you they can stay. We stand there & watch as they look through the drawers, try on our clothes, begin answering to our names.

(VII)

From what I understood, the ghosts had always been volatile. When you & I saw them again, fumbling with the iron latch on the gate, we noticed a change in the weather. The house grew colder & colder. Soon the ice became too much, sealing the windows & every door. By then we had already started shivering & the furniture was covered in frost. Spring came, but none of the rooms ever thawed, so we decided we'd generate our own heat. That was the beginning of our marriage, which seemed to keep the ghosts from picking up the knives.

(VIII)

Even when you kept stalling, smoking a cigarette on stairs, I knew the ghosts were watching. They took notes & filed them away in cabinets, one by one, our secrets each in their proper compartment. I tried to look once, but the drawers were locked, the key hidden somewhere I'd never be able to guess. Before, when the ghosts arrived, we had treated them as royalty, bringing them hors d'oeuvres & drinks. But now you & I knew better. We would do our best to calm them, since the curtains were scorched & the floor was already covered in ash.

(IX)

From the start, I knew that our marriage was one of practicality. You always said beauty can be a form of service. So every night, the ghosts would watch me straighten my dress, fasten my veil & button my long silk gloves. For awhile, it kept them from looting the armoire, or worse, starting those small fires in the vestibule. I did what I could to keep the house from burning. Soon they see me all shimmering in white & can barely speak. You just stand there & stare, your suit covered in ash, the altar catching fire behind you.

(X)

You were never quite sure about my dress, the way its cold silk trailed through the city below. Still I'd fasten the veil, straighten my sleeves & button those long white gloves. I waited & waited, but you never seemed to make up your mind. The fire grew smaller & the room darker. My dress was smudged with soot. Before long I'd see a flash of light in the doorway, the groom everyone else was afraid of. That's what I loved about you. Somehow you just stand there, a handkerchief folded in your front pocket, the room burning all around you.

(XI)

One night, after you'd finished tending the fire, you told me the truth about the ghosts.   They had been the smallest stars in a grand constellation, which lit the streets in the city below.   Then piece by piece, the sky darkened. The stars held their breath & before long they felt the weight of their clothes shifting.   Their dresses crackled with frost. That was when they began walking from house to house, fumbling with the silver locks on every door. You recognized them only by the cold light shining from each of their perfectly shaped mouths.

(XII)

From the very beginning, I loved you in spite of the ghosts. I'd watch you washing their dishes, picking up their clothes, trying to learn each of their names. It felt strange to see them giving orders, the lords & ladies of a small manor. Still you handed them napkins, asked about their mothers. Before the ghosts, you & I had thought about having children of our own, but they inevitably took over. The house was covered in ash. But even then I learned to like them, since you & I could see each other by the white light shining in every room.

(XIII)

You had an odd way of showing affection. Trembling &
out of breath, you'd appear in the doorway, hauling those
cold dead stars in their caskets. You always looked as
though you'd carried them a long way in the snow. But I
couldn't let you inside, not until you'd buried each of the
constellations. That's when you begin reciting their
names one by one. At that point there isn't much I can
do. I unlock the gates, open the front door, set the dining
room table. You walk in as though you've been knighted,
your lords & ladies trailing behind you.

(XIV)

Even when they became unruly, tearing at the floorboards & our furniture, I never expected the ghosts to drive us apart. The change was slow at first. You started sleeping with your eyes half-closed, watching the window for signs. Then sleep came upon me like a breath of winter air, & I woke to an empty bed, your magnificent suit in pieces on the floor. I realized you weren't my husband any more than I had been your wife. That same day, I saw you standing in the vestibule, but even the light around your eyes was gone.

(XV)

When you left that night, holding those dark red stars in your hand, I knew you weren't coming back. But I'd still set the table, lay out the silverware & wait in the vestibule. After the food grew cold, I'd open & close the windows, watch the sky as she burned through her dress. For weeks the room grew colder & the windows shone brighter. By then I was sure there was nothing that could be done. I closed the gate, locked the door, & cleared away the dishes. Somehow I keep expecting you to appear, your hands scorched & your suit covered in ash.

(XVI)

You left & the ghosts arrived, dragging their lamps & the last of the kerosene. I let them in, one by one, taking their long black coats. The house reeks of smoke. Now they're unlacing their boots & sitting down at the table. I serve them dinner on little silver plates, but they pick at their food, feed the hors d'oeuvres to the dog. I try & try to please them. That's when they gather all the photographs, my books, our wedding album. It's safe to say they didn't expect me to light the first match. Before I know it, we've started another fire.

(XVII)

Soon the ghosts started looking through the drawers, taking an inventory of what they've found. I tried to tell them they were only guests, but they kept picking the locks, emptying out the clothes, the silverware & all the dishes. They looked at each other as though they'd come into an inheritance, the funeral finally behind them. By then there wasn't much that could be done. I let them keep the broken plates, the torn handkerchiefs, & each of the spoons. They looked right past me as I held out the last of the silk napkins, offering what I could.

(XVIII)

Before long, the ghosts became a burden, keeping me up at night with their arguments & those small fires in the vestibule. I asked them to keep quiet, made them tea & cocoa, but realized they never slept. They rioted & banged on my bedroom door. The evenings grew shorter & the days longer. Soon I could barely hold my eyes open, started each morning with espresso. But what I missed most were the dreams. I realized you were really gone, since I'd never see you when I slept, hauling those iced-over stars behind you.

(XIX)

After a week had passed, I wondered why you left me alone with the ghosts. They seemed harmless at first, riffling through the drawers & each of the cupboards. But they couldn't stay away from the knives for very long. Before I knew it they'd slit all of the drapes down the middle, cut the sofa cushions wide open. They slept with those silver utensils next to their beds, turned in the middle of the night to make sure they were still there. Every morning they greeted me with that cold radiance, & I was unsure if the light was a promise or a threat.

(XX)

After you'd been gone a few months, I found a plain white envelope in our mailbox. Crumpled & frosted-over, it had been postmarked the night you left. I didn't recognize the name of the city, but I knew it was somewhere north of here. For weeks, I kept the letter folded in my shirt pocket, pictured you carrying those helpless stars through the snow. I could already feel the sky burning through the ice on my dress. But nothing else seemed to change. I tore into the envelope & there was only winter inside, not even a card or a handwritten note.

(XXI)

The next morning, I gathered all of the things you'd left behind: a tie rack, a black umbrella, some candies still in their box. I place each one of them on a mahogany shelf, record their height in a dark red book. You've left me enough trinkets for a thrift store, but I feel the same sky burning. Soon I hear a voice calling from the other room, warning me about the weather. It's always the smallest things that put me on edge. I begin to feel uneasy in this elaborate dress. That's when I strike a match & light the house on fire. Some days it's like you never left.

(XXII)

That night you came home, you didn't understand why I was surprised. We hadn't seen each other in years. Even when you'd approach me, dragging those dark red stars behind you, I could never look for very long. I started to remember the open windows, water drenching the curtains & spilling onto the floor. Now the sky has been lit & I can't stop thinking about the weather. It's always the strangest things that make me feel restless. Still you just stand there, light shimmering in your hair, the room catching fire all around you.

APPENDIX A:
ILLUSTRATIONS

FIGURE 1.

FIGURE 2.

FIGURE 3.

APPENDIX B:
WHAT SURVIVED THE FIRES

You began.   Then   night   &

                  I could hardly speak.

The next morning,
           a broken window, my
chandelier   in a locked box.

The armoire
is covered in soot.

That cold light gathering all around us.
We stand there & watch

the ghosts
fumbling with the

the ice.

The mirror   was covered in frost.

That was the beginning of   marriage,

the key hidden somewhere

the curtains   scorched & the floor   smudged with
   ash.

You
 would watch me straighten my dress,   my veil &

         start   those small fires in the vestibule. I
did what I could to keep the house from

      the

      cold.

     The fire grew smaller but

that's what I loved about you.

                                    You told me the truth
about   the   stars

                            & piece by piece, the sky
darkened. The stars

                        crackled with frost.

        That cold light shining from each of their
                mouths.

                    I loved you in spite of the ghosts

            but they inevitably took over.

                            Trembling & out of
breath, you

                looked as though you'd carried them
a long way in the snow. But I couldn't

            unlock the gates.

I never expected the ghosts to drive us apart.

A breath of winter air, & I woke

that same day

holding those dark red stars in my hand.

It's safe to say you didn't expect me
to

let you keep the broken plates, the
torn handkerchiefs, & each of the spoons.

What I missed most were the dreams,
        since I'd never see you   hauling
those iced-over stars behind you.

        I wondered why you left me alone.

        I kept the letter   in my
    pocket,

        but nothing   seemed to change.
There was only winter inside, not even

        trinkets

or a match.   It   was   like   you   never left.

Appendix C:
Notes & Observations

*

I became aware of your voice calling me from the stairs,
warning me about the silver lock on the door—

*

I hardly listened. When I arrived you placed a curiously
white envelope in my shaking hand—

*

The room was never empty. But in order for there to be a ghost in the house, someone had to have died—

*

Your brief materialization, a cold white star in the kitchen window. And my heartbeat, once or twice felt, with a sigh of feigned content—

*

One by one dishes filled the sink. There was always that sad film being projected against a white screen—

*

But there are other kinds of memory. More often than not, a magnificent exhaustion. Then one by one the stars—

*

My desire to romanticize, I realized, had been a form of grief. Still the luminous buttons on your shirt—

*

Once opened, I placed the curiously clean-looking letter
inside a locked box—

*

More than anything, the ghosts were loyal. They never asked what the I kept inside that towering white armoire—

*

At first I wondered why they chose us. But after awhile I knew. It was that cold light shining from every open window—

*

I tried & tried to please them. But either way everything
in the house would be covered in ash—

*

Still I wondered how you could ever leave, to live as a king without his court, without his crown—

NOTES ON THE TEXT.

The images provided in Appendix A (Figures 1, 2, and 3) depict several different astronomical clocks, which show the relative location of the sun and the moon. Appendix B consists of erasures of poems that appeared earlier in the manuscript.

ABOUT THE AUTHOR.

Kristina Marie Darling is the author of seventeen books, which include *Melancholia (An Essay)* (Ravenna Press, 2012), *Petrarchan* (BlazeVOX Books, 2013), and a forthcoming hybrid genre collection called *Fortress* (Sundress Publications, 2014). Her awards include fellowships from Yaddo, the Helene Wurlitzer Foundation, and the Hawthornden Castle International Retreat for Writers, as well as grants from the Kittredge Fund and the Elizabeth George Foundation. She is currently working toward a Ph.D. in Poetics at S.U.N.Y.-Buffalo.

25984358R00044

Made in the USA
Middletown, DE
20 November 2015